Nelson Comprehension

Pupil Book 2

OXFORD
UNIVERSITY PRESS

OXFORD
UNIVERSITY PRESS

Great Clarendon Street, Oxford, OX2 6DP, United Kingdom

Oxford University Press is a department of the University of Oxford.
It furthers the University's objective of excellence in research, scholarship,
and education by publishing worldwide. Oxford is a registered trade mark of
Oxford University Press in the UK and in certain other countries

First published by Nelson Thornes Ltd in 2009
This edition published by Oxford University Press in 2020

British Library Cataloguing in Publication Data
Data available

ISBN: 978-1-38-201429-8

5 7 9 10 8 6

Paper used in the production of this book is a natural, recyclable product
made from wood grown in sustainable forests. The manufacturing
process conforms to the environmental regulations of the country of origin.

Printed in China by Shanghai Offset Printing Products Ltd

Acknowledgements
Cover illustration: Nigel Kitching

Illustrations: Jim Eldridge, Mike Lacey, Wes Lowe, Matt Ward, Claire Mumford, Pedro Penizzotto,
Mike Phillips (all c/o Beehive Illustration), Topics, pp.6–7: Nigel Kitching, pp.8–9: Victor Tavares/
Beehive Illustration, pp.16–17: Sole Otero, pp.34–37: John Prater, pp.34–37, pp.44–45: Anjan Sarkar.

Photographs: p10: Nicholas Yarsley; p11(t): Nicholas Yarsley; p11(b): Fotolia; p12: Nicholas Yarsley;
p13: belchonock / 123RF; p18-19: Fotolia; p30(t): Ermolaev Alexander / Shutterstock; p30-31: Fotolia;
p32-33: Fotolia; p38: Fotolia; p40(t): Jo Ann Snover / 123RF; p40(m): Paul Daniels / Shutterstock;
p41(t): Christopher Futcher / iStock; p41(b): Fotolia.

The author and publisher are grateful to the following for permission to reprint copyright material:

Heather Amery: extract from 'Little Red Riding Hood' from The Usborne Book of Fairy Tales (Usborne,
2004), copyright © Usborne Publishing Ltd 2004, reprinted by permission of Usborne Publishing,
83-85 Saffron Hill, London EC1N 8RT, www.usborne.com; Bernard Ashley: extracts from A Present
for Paul (Collins, 1996), reprinted by permission of HarperCollins Publishers Ltd; Brigid Avison:
extract from I Wonder Why My Tummy Rumbles: and other questions about my body (Kingfisher, 2002),
copyright © Kingfisher Publications, 1993, reprinted by permission of Macmillan Publishers Ltd;
Marie Voigt: extracts from Red and the City (Oxford University Press, 2018), text and illustration
copyright © Marie Voigt 2018; and extracts from Jazz Dog (Oxford University Press, 2019), text and
illustration copyright © Marie Voigt 2019, reprinted by permission of Oxford University Press;
John Foster: 'Leap Like a Leopard' from Doctor Proctor and Other Rhymes (OUP, 1998), copyright ©
John Foster 1998, reprinted by permission of the author; Susan Gates: extract from Jellyfish Shoes
(OUP, 2014), copyright © Susan Gates 1998, reprinted by permission of David Higham Associates;
Paddy Kinsale: extract from 'Making Pancakes When My Mother Was Out' from Bandwagon edited
by Barry Maybury (OUP, 1974), reprinted by permission of Valerie Maybury; Eve Merriam: 'Catch a
Little Rhyme' from Catch a Little Rhyme (Atheneum, 1966), reprinted by permission of Marian Reiner,
Literary Agent.

Oxford OWL
Discover eBooks, inspirational
resources, advice and support
www.oxfordowl.co.uk

Contents

		Scope and Sequence	4
Unit	1	Familiar Settings	6
Unit	2	Instructions	10
Unit	3	Traditional Stories	14
Unit	4	Explanations	18
Unit	5	Patterns on the Page	22
Unit	6	Different Stories, Same Author	26
Unit	7	Finding Facts	30
Unit	8	Extended Stories	34
Unit	9	Understanding Information Texts	38
Unit	10	Poetry	42
		How to Use This Book	46

Scope and Sequence

Unit	Unit Focus	Texts	Oxford Level	Oxford Reading Criterion Scale	Genre / text type
I	Familiar Settings	*Making Pancakes When My Mother Was Out*, Paddy Kinsale	I0	standard 3, criteria 7, 20, 2I, 23	fiction and settings
		A Present for Paul, Bernard Ashley	II		
2	Instructions	Make a Mess!	8	standard 3, criteria 6, I0, 20, 25, 26	instructions
		Making Butter	8		
3	Traditional Stories	*Little Red Riding Hood*	8	standard 3, criteria 7, 8, 9, I8, 20, 2I, 22, 23	modern and traditional fairy tales
		Little Red Riding Hood, Heather Amery	8		
4	Explanations	*All About Me*	N/A	standard 3, criteria 8, 9, I0, II, I8, 20, 25, 26, 29	non-fiction
		What Does My Heart Do? Brigid Avison	9		
5	Patterns on the Page	'Catch a Little Rhyme', Eve Merriam	9	standard 3, criteria 20, 2I, 23	poetry
		'Leap Like a Leopard', John Foster	9		
6	Different Stories, Same Author	*Red and the City*, Marie Voigt	II	standard 3, criteria I7, 20, 2I, 23	different fiction stories by same author
		Jazz Dog, Marie Voigt	II		
7	Finding Facts	Cats	9	standard 3, criteria 6, I0, 20, 24, 25, 26	non-fiction
		Pet Cat Facts	9		
8	Extended Stories	*Jellyfish Shoes*, Susan Gates	I0	standard 3, criteria 7, 20, 2I, 23	longer fiction stories
		'The Shoes Come Back!' from *Jellyfish Shoes*, Susan Gates	I0		
9	Understanding Information Texts	Adventure World	9	standard 3, criteria 5, 6, I0, 20, 25, 26	non-fiction posters and planning
		Planning a Day Out	9		
I0	Poetry	'I Wonder', Jeannie Kirby	8	standard 3, criteria 20, 2I, 23	poetry
		'Ice Lolly', Pie Corbett	8		

Resources & Assessment Book Support	Resources & Assessment Book Extension
completing sentences	predicting what happens next; describing and drawing
putting sentences into correct order	circling correct answers; writing about own experiences
putting pictures into correct order	making a list; writing instructions
circling the correct answer; writing explanations	writing instructions
describing characters	writing about what happens next
identifying true and false statements	comparing traditional tales
finding words in index and writing them in order	answering comprehension questions
matching words to their definition	researching information
cloze activity	answering questions and explaining opinions
cloze activity	completing a table and explaining opinions
describing Red	writing a book review
writing and ordering sentences	comparing stories
answering literal comprehension questions	adding further information
linking lines to complete sentences	writing about page layouts
putting sentences into correct order	answering questions with full sentences
writing about characters' feelings	predicting what happens next
underlining correct answers	explaining information
listing and writing about ideas	planning a day out
cloze activity	writing activity
looking more closely at the poem; answering questions	planning and writing a poem

UNIT 1

Making Pancakes When My Mother Was Out

Some friends decided to make pancakes because Mum had said she didn't have time. They thought it would save her the trouble …

We got out a big dish and I climbed on a stool and reached the flour down from the cupboard, knocking the sugar over as I did it. That was the first accident. You know what sugar's like – it seems to get all over the place – in the bread and butter, all over the floor, and some of it was on Ruthie's head. She didn't mind. She was licking it up as it trickled down her face.

We put some flour in the dish and scraped the sugar into it off the table. There were a few bread crumbs as well but we didn't think it would matter very much because, as Bill said, bread was made from flour anyway. Then Sally broke some eggs into it and dropped one on the floor. I was just going for the floor-cloth to get it up when Ruthie went and stood on it.

'Naughty girl!' I said, and she started to cry and backed away, bumping into Bill who was just taking the top off a bottle of milk so that it jerked his hand and the milk went everywhere, most of it all over my back, because I was kneeling down trying to get the egg up.

'I've got half an eggshell in this,' Sally said. 'I can't get it out.' She was trying to fish it out with a pencil, and the more she fished the further it got stuck in the goo.

Paddy Kinsale

Teach

1 What do the friends decide to make?

2 What happens when the flour is taken from the cupboard?

3 What does Sally drop on the floor?

4 Why is Ruthie told off?

5 What is the pencil used for?

Look carefully at the first paragraph.

6 Which word in the text tells us that the children had not planned to make a mess?

7 How do we know, at the beginning of the story, there is going to be more than one accident?

8 Why does the narrator call Ruthie a 'naughty girl'?

9 Which of the children do you think is the youngest?

10 What do you think Mum is going to say when she comes home? Add five sentences to continue the story.

Talk

Where's Dad?

Pleasure and her dad went to the market. Pleasure wanted to get a present for her baby brother, Paul.

It was all bustle and bags when they got off the bus. And Dad with all that shopping to do.

'Vegetables,' he said, holding her tightly.

And he bought chillies, potatoes and beans.

But Pleasure was eyeing the children's stall.

'I want to get something for Paul.' …

And her hand went straight to her pocket when her father let go to pay. Because over there was a teething ring – just right for the baby to bite.

… She was thinking how pleased the baby would be – but the smile was wiped off in a flash.

'Dad … !'

Because her dad wasn't there anymore!

He wasn't there?

Where was he?

She'd only just turned round, how could he have gone so quick? She twisted back the other way – but he wasn't there either, only strangers' legs and their coats and their bags.

There was everyone else, but no sign of him!

Her stomach did a head over heels – but he always said she was a big girl, so she wasn't going to get scared!

A Present for Paul, **Bernard Ashley**

Copy the right answers.

1 Who is Pleasure thinking about?

Pleasure is thinking about her baby brother Paul.

Pleasure is thinking about her mum.

2 Why did Pleasure suddenly feel worried?

Pleasure had lost her money.   Pleasure had lost her dad.

3 What did Pleasure's dad always call her?

He called her his big girl.   He called her his little girl.

The text uses some interesting phrases.

4 It says Pleasure's smile was 'wiped off in a flash'.

What does 'wiped off in a flash' mean?

5 It says that Pleasure's stomach did a 'head over heels'.

What does 'head over heels' mean?

6 How do you think Pleasure feels when she arrives at the market?

7 How do you think Pleasure feels when she gets lost?

Copy the words that tell us how Pleasure might be feeling.

happy   sad   worried   pleased   scared

bright   upset   frightened   jolly   tearful

8 Have you ever been lost or felt very frightened?

How did it feel?

Write about how you felt.

Write

9

Make a Mess!

You will need:

washing-up liquid

a glass jar

clear vinegar

glitter

food dye

bicarbonate of soda

a teaspoon

What to do:

1 Half fill the jar with the vinegar.

2 Add a teaspoon of food dye and a teaspoon of glitter.

3 Add a big squeeze of washing-up liquid, then stir carefully.

4 Add a heaped teaspoon of bicarbonate of soda.

5 Watch what happens!

Warning!
This is NOT a drink.

Look at the instructions.

1 What do you have to do first?

2 What do you add at the same time as the glitter?

3 How much washing-up liquid do you add?

4 What does the last instruction ask you to do?

5 Why are these things used?

The first one has been done for you.

a washing-up liquid   This makes the mess bubble!

b food dye

c glass jar

d glitter

6 Think about how the instructions are written.

In what order do you find these?
Warning   You will need: Title   What to do:

7 Make a list of different things we need instructions for.

8 Choose one thing you have listed and write what you would need to do it.

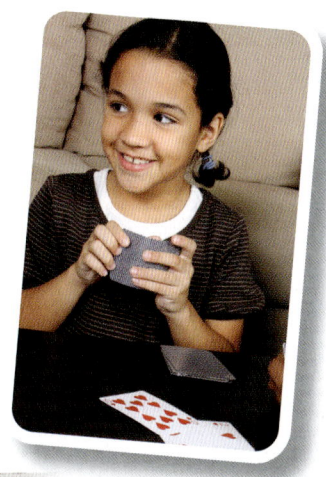

Making Butter

You will need:

some paper towels   a clean jar with a lid

a bowl

a sieve

500 ml of double cream or full-fat milk

What to do:

1

2

3

4

5

1 Write out the instructions in the correct order.

- Shake the jar for 20 minutes (or more), until you have big lumps in the cream.
- Pour the cream into the jar and screw on the lid.
- Pour the contents from the jar into the sieve. The lumps are butter!
- Put the paper towel in the sieve and place it over the bowl.
- Put your butter in the fridge.

2 **Verbs** are usually doing words. They can tell us what people are doing.

Look at the instructions above and copy four different verbs.

3 Why is a sieve needed?

4 Which part of making butter do you think would be the hardest?

5 Why does a clean jar with a lid need to be used?

6 How do you make a jam sandwich?

Write your own instructions.

Little Red Riding Hood

Ruby loved the red hooded top her Granny gave her. She wore it everywhere. Soon people started to call her Little Red Riding Hood.

One morning, Little Red Riding Hood's mum was making cakes in the kitchen. Little Red Riding Hood had an idea.

'Mum,' she said, 'could I take some of your cakes and a drink to Granny? I'm sure she would love them.'

'What a good idea,' her mother said, 'and she'd like to see you too!'

Little Red Riding Hood got her bike ready, put on her helmet and set off.

'Remember, go straight to Granny's and don't talk to strangers,' shouted her mum.

Little Red Riding Hood passed her friends as she rode out of town. She loved riding to Granny's through the fields, away from the busy roads.

Suddenly, with no warning, a wolf leapt in front of Little Red Riding Hood. She had to brake very quickly.

'Watch out!' she yelled.

The wolf just smiled. 'Show me what is in your basket, little girl. Something smells very nice.'

Retold by **Sarah Lindsay**

Teach

1 Why was the girl called 'Little Red Riding Hood'?

2 What was Little Red Riding Hood taking to her granny?

3 Where did Little Red Riding Hood meet the wolf?

4 What did the wolf want?

5 Is Little Red Riding Hood a 'good' or 'bad' character in the story?

6 What words would you use to describe Little Red Riding Hood?

7 Is the wolf a 'good' or 'bad' character in the story?

8 What words would you use to describe the wolf?

9 How do we know Little Red Riding Hood and her granny care for each other?

10 Finish this story. It can finish in any way you want.

   What happened next?

Talk

Little Red Riding Hood

Little Red Riding Hood and her mother live near a big, dark forest.

Her name comes from a bright red cloak with a hood that her granny made her.

'Please take this food to your granny. She's unwell in bed,' says her mother. 'Go through the forest but don't talk to any strangers you meet on the way.'

Little Red Riding Hood waves goodbye.

She walks into the forest with her basket. She doesn't see the Big Black Wolf watching her from behind a tree.

Suddenly the Wolf is on the path.

'Where are you going?' he asks.

'I'm taking this food to Granny,' says Red Riding Hood, feeling very scared.

Heather Amery

Write

Copy and finish the sentences.

1 Granny made Little Red Riding Hood's _____.

basket   cloak   cake

2 Little Red Riding Hood's granny felt _____.

unwell   happy   tired

3 Little Red Riding Hood walked through the _____.

field   village   forest

4 Little Red Riding Hood was scared of the _____.

forest   wolf   dark

5 **Adjectives** are describing words.

Copy the adjectives used to describe these nouns.

a the forest

b the cloak

c the wolf

6 You have now read the start of two Little Red Riding Hood stories.

a List what is different about the two stories.

b List what is the same about the two stories.

7 Which story do you prefer?

Write a sentence to say why.

Write

Finding Information

Index

B

blinking	18
bones	4, 8–9
brain	4, 7, 20–21
burping	25

C

cramp	13

D

dreaming	27

E

ears	6, 12

H

hair	5, 10
heart	4, 16–17
hiccups	25

M

mouth	22

N

nose	22

S

skin	4, 24
sleeping	21, 27

T

tears	18
teeth	22

W

windpipe	14, 15

Teach

Look at the front cover.

1   What is the book about?

2   Who wrote the book?

Look at the index.

3   What is an index used for?

4   On what pages would you find information on the heart?

5   On what page would you find information on teeth?

6   **Nouns** are naming words.

List five nouns found in the index.

7   Sleeping can be found on page 27.

What else can be found on this page? Why?

8   On which page do you think there would be information on 'Why do I blink'?

9   Look up information on eyes.

Can you fill in these missing labels?

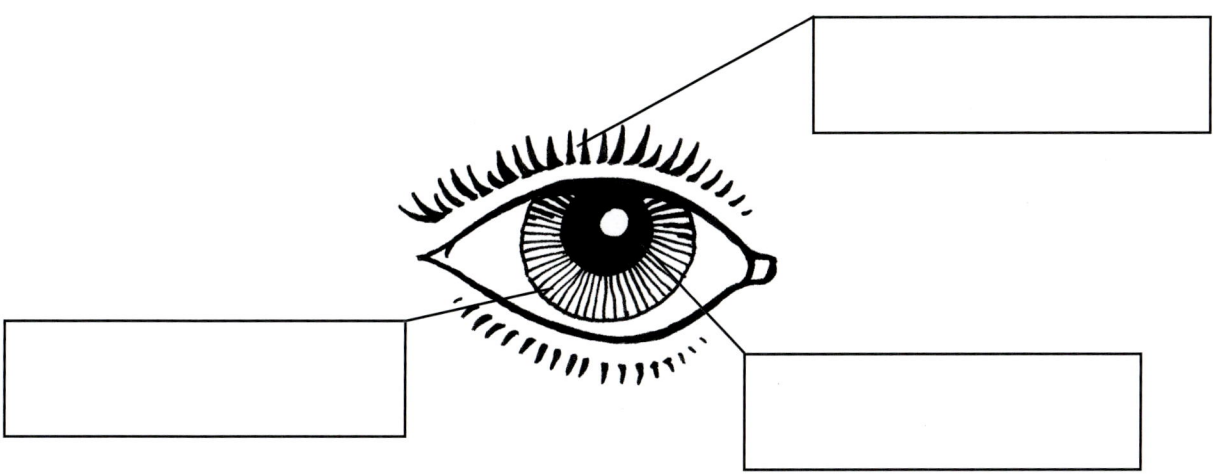

Talk

What Does My Heart Do?

heart

Your heart is a very special muscle which keeps blood moving around your body. If you put your hand on your chest near your heart, you'll feel it beating. Each time it beats, it pumps blood out around your body.

To hear a heart beating, find somewhere quiet and rest your ear against a friend's chest. You should hear two sounds close together – 'lub-dub', 'lub-dub', 'lub-dub'.

How big is my heart?
Our hearts grow with us – they get bigger as we do. Whatever size you are now, your heart will be a bit bigger than your fist.

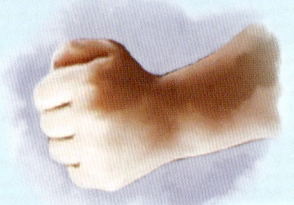

I Wonder Why My Tummy Rumbles, **Brigid Avison**

Copy and complete the sentences.

1 The heart is a _____.

bone   muscle

2 The heart pumps _____ around your body.

water   blood

3 The heart makes _____ sounds close together.

two   four

4 Your heart is a bit _____ than your fist.

bigger   smaller

5 A **glossary** is a list of special words and their explanations.
It is written in alphabetical order.

a b c d e f g h i j k l m n o p q r s t u v w x y z

| heart   a muscle that pumps blood around a body |

a Choose five words from the page that could go in a glossary.

b Write the words you have chosen in alphabetical order.

6 List two facts that you think people may not know about
the heart.

7 Choose a part of your body.
Find out about it.
You could:
• look in books
• look on a computer
• ask friends and adults questions
Draw the body part and write about what you have found out.

Write

UNIT
5

Catch a Little Rhyme

Once upon a time
I caught a little rhyme

I set it on the floor
but it ran right out the door

I chased it on my bicycle
but it melted to an icicle

I scooped it up in my hat
but it turned into a cat

I caught it by the tail
but it stretched into a whale

I followed it in a boat
but it changed into a goat

When I fed it tin and paper
it became a tall skyscraper

Then it grew into a kite
and flew far out of sight ...

Eve Merriam

Teach

1 When the rhyme was put on the floor where did it run?

2 Where was the rhyme when it turned into a cat?

3 What did the rhyme stretch into?

4 What had the rhyme been fed when it became a skyscraper?

5 Some of the words in the poem **rhyme**.

Find the words that each of these words rhyme with.

boat   time   bicycle   floor   kite   tail

6 This poem is about someone who is trying to catch a rhyme.

How do you think this person is feeling?

7 Read the poem again.

  a Do you like it? Why?
  b Does it make you smile? Why?

Leap Like a Leopard

Leap like a leopard.
Hop like a kangaroo.
Swing from branch to branch
Like a monkey in a zoo.

Dive like a dolphin.
Plunge like a whale.
Creep like a caterpillar.
Crawl like a snail.

Scuttle like a spider.
Slither like a snake.
Slide like a duck
On a frozen lake.

Skip like a lamb.
Jump like a frog.
Stalk like a cat.
Scamper like a dog.

John Foster

Write

Copy the right answers.

1 What does the kangaroo do?

The kangaroo leaps.　　The kangaroo hops.

2 Where does the monkey swing?

The monkey swings in a zoo.

The monkey swings at the playground.

3 What slides on a frozen lake?

A snake slides.　　A duck slides.

4 What does the cat do?

The cat walks.　　The cat stalks.

Look at the poem.

5 Which word rhymes with 'kangaroo'?

6 Which word rhymes with 'whale'?

7 Which word rhymes with 'snake'?

8 Which word rhymes with 'frog'?

9 Look carefully at the poem.

　a What is the poem about?

　b Write the words that are repeated.

10 Now look at both of the poems in this unit.

　a What do you like and what don't you like about the poems?

　b Which poem do you prefer?

Write

UNIT 6

Red and the City

Once there was a girl named Red, who lived with her mum and her dog, Woody, on the edge of the city.

'Red,' said her mum one day. 'Go visit Grandma and give her this cake. Take Woody with you and remember—

Follow the heart flowers . . .
take care when crossing the road . . .
stay on the path . . .
and don't talk to anyone.'

After a while, Red started feeling hungry.
'I will only have a little bit of cake,' Red said.
But the cake was very tasty.
And before Red knew it,
she'd eaten it all.

'Oh no, I've eaten my present for Grandma,' said Red. 'What shall I do now? I know! I'll buy her some heart flowers. They're not far from the path. I'll be back in a minute.'

But Red quickly forgot about the flowers . . .

Red and the City, **Marie Voigt**

1 Who did Red live with?

2 What is Red asked to do?

3 Why does Red eat the cake?

4 What type of flowers does Red decide to get for her Grandma?

5 Which of these words could be used to describe Red's mum? Why?

thoughtful   sad   caring

hungry   kind   worried

6 Can you think of any more words to describe Red's mum?

7 What do you like about the story?

8 What don't you like about the story?

9 Now write a review of a book you have enjoyed reading.

Remember to include:

- the title
- the author
- where the story is set
- what happens
- who the main characters are
- why your friends should read it

Talk

Jazz Dog

Amongst the loud and POWERFUL Rock Dogs, there was one dog who played differently.

His music didn't sound like theirs, and he just couldn't find a place where he fitted in . . . until one night, a place found him.

The dog listened in awe to the BEAUTIFUL sound of the Jazz Cats.

He stayed all night long, then he made up his mind.

'I want to learn your sound,' he said to the cat.

But the cat pointed to a sign. 'Sorry, DOGS OUT!' he said. And he slammed the door shut.

The dog practised cat jazz all day and all night, even though everyone laughed and said, 'But dogs should play rock!'

He knew in his heart though that his music was right.

And he dreamed of cats and dogs playing together some day.

Write

Jazz Dog, **Marie Voigt**

Copy the right answers.

1 What music did the dog want to learn to play?

The dog wanted to learn to play music like the Rock Dogs.

The dog wanted to learn to play music like the Jazz Cats.

2 Why was the dog different from the other Rock Dogs?

His music didn't sound like theirs.

He didn't play any music.

Answer each question with a sentence.

3 Who slammed the door shut on the dog?

4 What did the dog dream of?

5 Which words in the text tell you how long the dog practised cat jazz for?

6 *Red and the City* and *Jazz Dog* are written by the same author, Marie Voigt.

a Write a list of the things that are similar in both stories.

b Write a list of the things that are different in both stories.

7 Which story did you like more?

 *Red and the City*  *Jazz Dog*

Write a sentence saying why.

Write

UNIT
7

Cats

- There are many different kinds of cat.
- Did you know that the big wild cats are related to the cats that live in our homes?
- All cats eat meat.
- Cats have good eyesight and a good sense of smell.

Pet cats

These cats live with people. They don't have to hunt for their food, but sometimes they catch birds or mice.

Lions

These cats live in groups called 'prides'. The male lions often relax while the lionesses do most of the hunting.

Tigers

These are the biggest cats. They like water, which most other cats don't like. They are good swimmers and often relax in the water to cool down.

Cheetahs

These are the fastest cats.
The cheetah is the fastest-running animal in the world.

Teach

1 Are wild cats related to pet cats?

2 What do tigers sometimes do
  to cool down?

3 Which are the biggest cats?

4 What do all cats eat?

5 Look each of these words up
  in a dictionary.

  Do any of these words have more
  than one meaning?

  pride   relax   tiger

Remember, a dictionary is set out in alphabetical order.

6 Look at the sections.

  In which section do we read about:

  a the male cat relaxing?

  b the cats not having to hunt for food?

  c the cats that enjoy swimming?

  d the fastest cats?

7 Read the information in the sections Pet cats, Lions, Tigers and
  Cheetahs again.

  a Write one or two of your own sentences to add to each section.

  b Can you think of any other type of cat? Write a sentence about it.

Talk

Pet Cat Facts

Cats sometimes eat grass. This can help them cough up hair balls.

Most cats like being brushed.

Cats need to scratch to exercise their muscles.

Cats wash themselves for many hours every day.

If cats miaow when you are near, it can mean they want your attention.

Most cats give birth to four to six kittens, though sometimes they may have as many as twelve.

Cats usually purr when they are happy.

Cats and dogs can be best friends.

Kittens play with moving things. While they are playing they are learning to hunt.

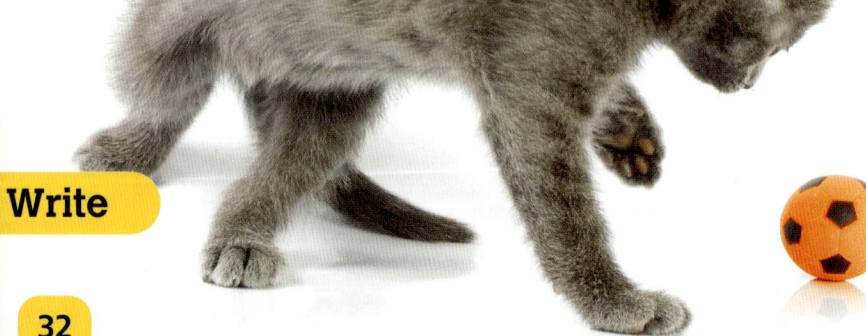

Write

Copy and finish the sentences.

1   Every day a cat will wash itself for _____.

minutes   hours

2   If a cat _____ it is happy.

purrs   miaows

Answer each question with a sentence.

3   Why do cats scratch?

4   Do cats like being brushed?

5   What do kittens learn while they are playing?

Don't forget to use capital letters and full stops!

6   Copy these words and their correct definitions.

attention   a band of tissue in a body that moves

muscle   a ball of hair

hair ball   to take notice

7   One fact tells us most cats like being brushed.
    Why do you think this is?

8   Look at the information on 'Cats' on page 30 and 'Cat facts' on page 32 again.

Write a sentence saying which is set out in the most helpful way.
Don't forget to say why.

Write

UNIT
8

Jellyfish Shoes

Laura had some new jelly shoes. She was really proud of them. They were pink and see-through like raspberry jelly. She ran down to the beach in them. Wherever she walked, they left little tracks in the sand. …

'Look, Scott,' Laura called to her brother. 'My new jelly shoes are leaving stars in the sand.'

Squidge. Laura trod in something slippery. She lifted up her shoe.

'Ughhh!' she said. 'What's that mess?'

It's only a jellyfish,' said Scott. 'The sea washes them up on the beach.'

'Well, I don't like it,' said Laura. 'It looks like a jelly cow-pat.' …

'I don't know why you hate jellyfish,' said Scott. 'What do you think your new shoes are made of?'

Laura looked down at her shoes. They were see-through and pink. The jellyfish on the beach were see-through and pink too.

'Don't be silly,' she told Scott. But her voice was shaky.

'I thought you knew,' said Scott. 'Don't you know what happens to all these washed-up jellyfish?'

Laura shook her head.

'I'll tell you what happens,' said Scott, who was good at stories. 'The jelly workers come round. They come round at night with bin bags. And they shovel all the jellyfish into the bags. And they take them away to the Jelly Shoe Factory.'

He went on, 'And they make them into shoes. Just like the ones you've got on. I thought everyone knew that!' …

'Yuk!' she said. 'I don't want pongy jellyfish shoes that sting me!'

She threw them into the sea.

Susan Gates

1 Does Laura like her new jelly shoes at the beginning of the story?

2 Who is Scott?

3 Why doesn't Laura like jellyfish?

4 Why did Laura throw her shoes in the sea?

5 Which words in the text describe Laura's jelly shoes?

6 What else in the story is described using the same words?

Read the story again.

7 Add three more notes to say what has happened so far.

- - Laura is pleased with her new jelly shoes.

- - Laura walks on the beach in her new shoes.

- - Laura shows her shoes to her brother.

- -

- -

- -

8 Are you enjoying the story so far?
Why?

9 Is there a line which makes you want to read more of the story?

Talk

The Shoes Come Back!

That night Laura dreamed about the jellyfish workers. ...

'Oh no!' cried Laura, waking up. 'The jelly workers are coming!'

But it was all right. She was safe in her own bed. 'It was just a bad dream,' she told herself.

Yet down on the dark beach, something was moving. Something was bobbing about on the waves. It was Laura's jellyfish shoes. They were coming back home.

Gently, they washed in on the wave tops until at last a big wave washed them up on the sand. Neatly side by side.

'What a bit of luck!' said Mum the next morning. 'Guess what I just found on the beach?'

'Don't know,' said Laura.

Mum held up the jellyfish shoes. 'These! I bet you didn't even know you'd lost them.'

Mum tipped up one of the shoes. A winkle fell out of the toe.

'Here you are,' she said, handing the shoes back to Laura. 'You can put them back on now.'

Laura pushed the shoes away: 'I won't put them back on!' she shouted. 'You can't make me!' ... 'Why did you do it, Mum? Why did you buy me shoes made of jellyfish?'

And Laura rushed out the door.

Mum shook her head, puzzled. 'Shoes made of jellyfish?' she said. 'What's she talking about? Do you know, Scott?'

'Don't ask me,' said Scott. But he looked a bit guilty.

Jellyfish Shoes, **Susan Gates**

Write

36

Copy and finish the sentences.

1 Laura had a _____ dream.

   good   bad

2 That night the _____ were washed up on the beach.

   jellyfish   jellyfish shoes

Answer with a sentence.

3 Who found Laura's jelly shoes?

4 Why didn't Laura want her shoes back?

5 Which word tells us Laura left in a hurry?

6 Which word tells us how Mum reacted when Laura
   didn't want her shoes?

Read the text again.

7 Why did Scott look guilty when his mum
   asked him why Laura was upset?

Scott looks for Laura and finds her on the
beach. He has two choices:

• He can tell her he made up the story.

• He can continue the story saying the
  jelly workers returned her shoes.

8 What do you think Scott says?

9 How does Laura react to what Scott says?

Adventure World

Come and discover our fantastic, fun, full-sized pirate ship with soft play island …

Terrific Trampolining

Sinking Sandpit

Swingboats

Tall Tree Houses

'Hours of fun, spend the day.'

'Loved by children of all ages.'

'One of the best adventure playgrounds ever!'

Open daily 10am to 4pm
(except Christmas Day)

Cost:
Children £5.00
Adults   £8.00

I was Captain Tuhil for the day. My friends and I had great fun capturing the island and making my brother walk the plank! I wish we could come back tomorrow.

Child-friendly café for tasty sandwiches, yummy fruit bowl, loads of sweets and delicious drinks.

Sorry, no dogs.
Children must be under 11 years and accompanied by an adult.

Teach

38

1 What is this leaflet about?

2 How much is a child's ticket for the day?

3 What can children do at the playground?

4 Do you need to bring a packed lunch?

5 Find three describing words that are used to persuade you to visit Adventure World, like **terrific**.

Look at Tuhil's comment.

6 Did Tuhil enjoy the day?

7 What did Tuhil play on?

8 Why do you think Tuhil's comment has been included in the leaflet?

9 Your family are deciding whether to go to the playground.

The leaflet gives you information on:
- what you can do there
- cost
- opening times
- comments from people who have visited the playground.

Why are each of these bits of information important?

Come to Adventure World!

Talk

Planning a Day Out

Where shall we go?

There are many exciting places to visit.
Some are linked with history, such as
castles and old houses.
Others are all about having fun, such as
adventure playgrounds and seaside piers.

How much will it cost?

Find out how much the day will cost.
Sometimes it is cheaper to buy a family
ticket instead of single tickets for
each person.
How much will it cost to get there?
Are there things to buy once you
are there?

How do we get there?

Spend time looking up how to get to
where you want to go.
It might save time on the day!
Often the website of the place will have
a map.

What shall we take?

Think about the clothes you wear.
Are they comfortable? Will they keep
you dry if it rains?
Do you need to take a packed lunch?
If it is a long day out, take
some snacks.
Remember to take some money.

Write

Copy and finish the sentences.

1 There are many _____ places to visit.

exciting   dull

2 Sometimes it is cheaper to buy a _____ ticket.

family   single

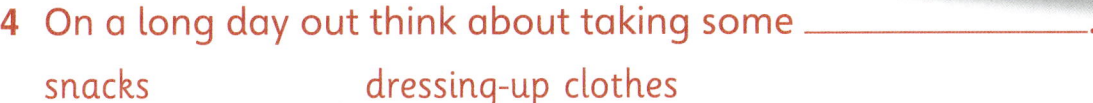

3 _____ often have a map to show how to get to a place.

Tickets   Websites

4 On a long day out think about taking some _____.

snacks   dressing-up clothes

5 Which word in the text tells us where piers are found?

6 Which word in the text tells us why it is better to buy a family ticket?

Answer each question with a sentence.

7 Which days out would you enjoy going on? Why?

8 List three things you may spend money on.

9 How would you choose what clothes to wear on a day out?

10 Look at the 'What shall we take?' section.

Write in note form what you need to take. The first two have been done for you.

- snacks
- trainers

You could use bullet points.

UNIT 10

I Wonder

I wonder why the grass is green,
And why the wind is never seen?

Who taught the birds to build a nest,
And told the trees to take a rest?

Or, when the moon is not quite round,
Where can the missing bit be found?

Who lights the stars, when they blow out,
And makes the lightning flash about?

Who paints the rainbow in the sky,
And hangs the fluffy clouds so high?

Why is it now, do you suppose,
That Dad won't tell me, if he knows?

Jeannie Kirby

Teach

What does the poet wonder?

1 Why is the grass … ?

2 Why is the moon … ?

3 Who lights the … ?

4 Who paints the … ?

5 Find a word in the poem that rhymes with …

nest	green	round
suppose	sky	out

6 Do you think 'Dad' knows the answers?

Read the poem again.

7 Do you like this poem? Why?

8 Do you have a favourite line?

Talk

UNIT 10

Ice Lolly

Red rocket
on a stick.
If it shines,
lick it quick.

Round the edges,
on the top,
round the bottom,
do not stop.
Suck the lolly,
lick your lips.

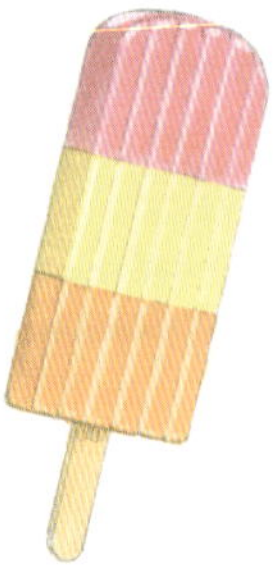

Lick the sides
as it drips
off the stick –
quick, quick,
lick, lick –
Red rocket
on a stick.

Pie Corbett

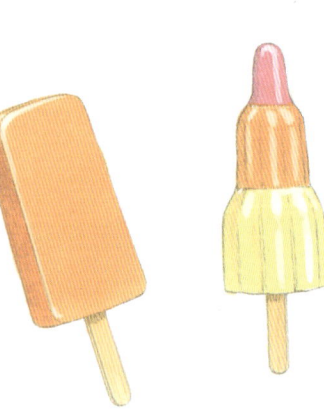

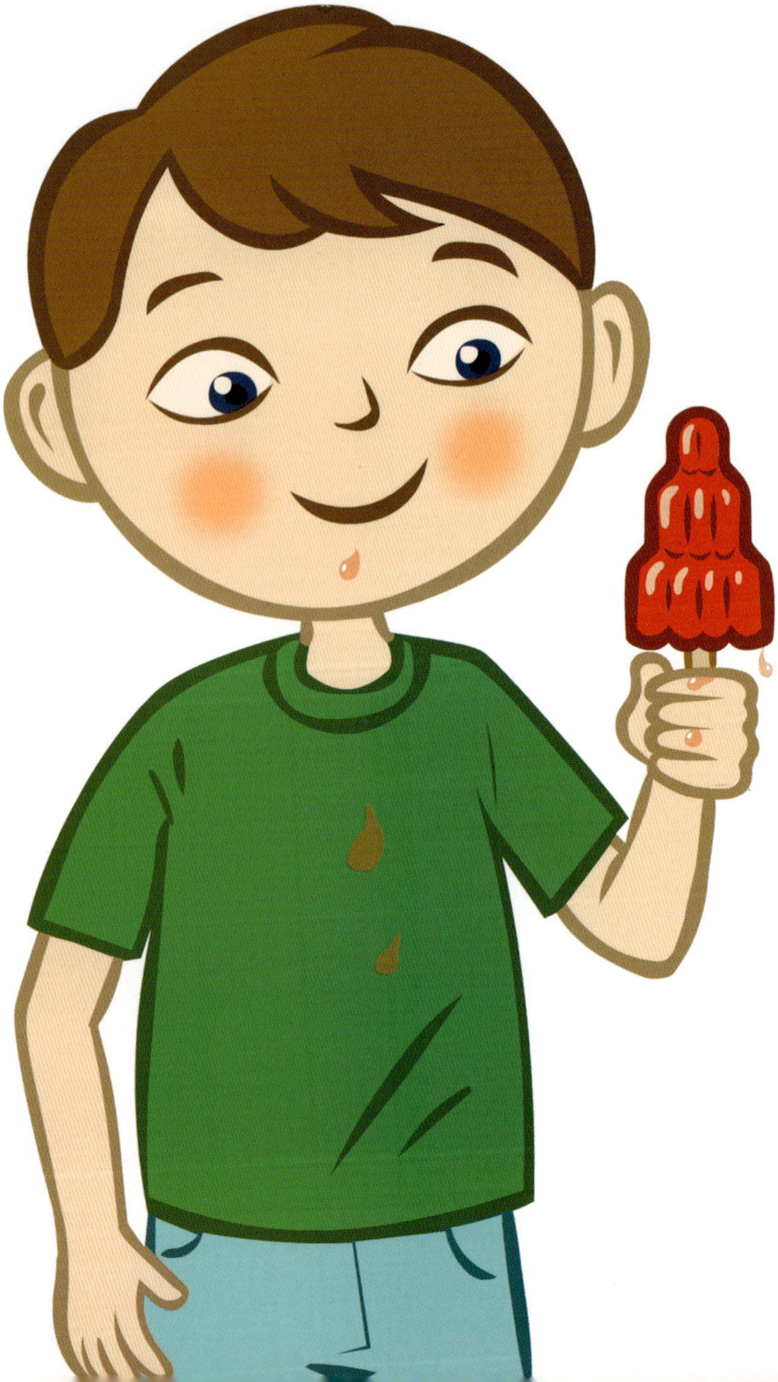

Write

Copy the right answers.

1 What is a 'red rocket'?

A red rocket is a lolly.   A red rocket is a stick.

2 Which part of the body does the poem say to lick?

The poem says to lick the hand.

The poem says to lick the lips.

Write a sentence to answer these questions.

3 How many times can you find 'lick' written in the poem?

4 Where does the poem say to lick the lolly?

There is more than one answer.

5 Which other words rhyme with 'lick'?

The poem says 'If it shines, lick it quick'.

6 Why do you think it says this?

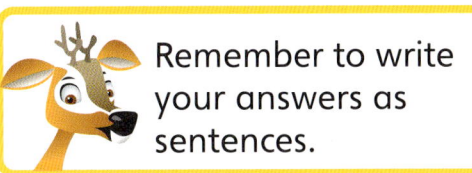

Remember to write your answers as sentences.

7 What else would you have to eat quickly in the sun?

8 Think of something else that is messy to eat.

Write your own short poem describing how to eat it.

Write

How to Use This Book

This heading tells you the name of the text.

The red questions are about understanding what's happened in the text.

This heading tells you about the unit topic.

The purple questions are about words and phrases used in the text.

Familiar Settings

Making Pancakes When My Mother Was Out

Some friends decided to make pancakes because Mum had said she didn't have time. They thought it would save her the trouble …

We got out a big dish and I climbed on a stool and reached the flour down from the cupboard, knocking the sugar over as I did it. That was the first accident. You know what sugar's like – it seems to get all over the place – in the bread and butter, all over the floor, and some of it was on Ruthie's head. She didn't mind. She was licking it up as it trickled down her face.

We put some flour in the dish and scraped the sugar into it off the table. There were a few bread crumbs as well but we didn't think it would matter very much because, as Bill said, bread was made from flour anyway. Then Sally broke some eggs into it and dropped one on the floor. I was just going for the floor-cloth to get it up when Ruthie went and stood on it.

'Naughty girl!' I said, and she started to cry and backed away, bumping into Bill who was just taking the top off a bottle of milk so that it jerked his hand and the milk went everywhere, most of it all over my back, because I was kneeling down trying to get the egg up.

'I've got half an eggshell in this,' Sally said. 'I can't get it out.' She was trying to fish it out with a pencil, and the more she fished the further it got stuck in the goo.

Paddy Kinsale

Teach

6

1 What do the friends decide to make?

2 What happens when the flour is taken from the cupboard?

3 What does Sally drop on the floor?

4 Why is Ruthie told off?

5 What is the pencil used for?

Look carefully at the first paragraph.

6 Which word in the text tells us that the children had not planned to make a mess?

7 How do we know, at the beginning of the story, there is going to be more than one accident?

8 Why does the narrator call Ruthie a 'naughty girl'?

9 Which of the children do you think is the youngest?

10 What do you think Mum is going to say when she comes home? Add five sentences to continue the story.

Talk

7

The author's name is here.

The green questions ask you to think more deeply about things from the text.

The blue questions ask you to think beyond the text.

Sometimes your teacher may ask you to fill in activity sheets.

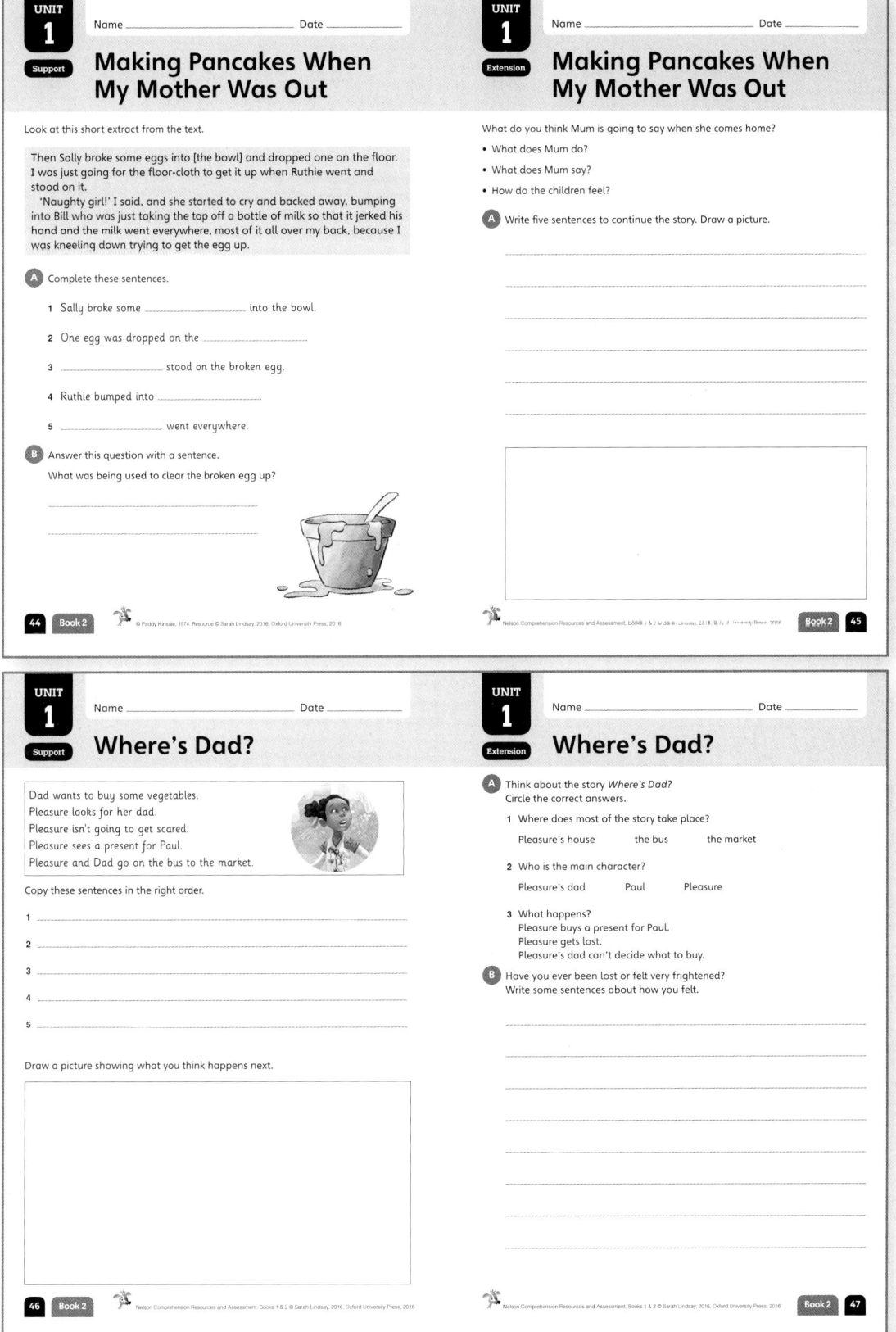

UNIT 1 Support

Name _____ Date _____

Making Pancakes When My Mother Was Out

Look at this short extract from the text.

Then Sally broke some eggs into [the bowl] and dropped one on the floor. I was just going for the floor-cloth to get it up when Ruthie went and stood on it.
'Naughty girl!' I said, and she started to cry and backed away, bumping into Bill who was just taking the top off a bottle of milk so that it jerked his hand and the milk went everywhere, most of it all over my back, because I was kneeling down trying to get the egg up.

A Complete these sentences.

1 Sally broke some _____ into the bowl.

2 One egg was dropped on the _____.

3 _____ stood on the broken egg.

4 Ruthie bumped into _____.

5 _____ went everywhere.

B Answer this question with a sentence.

What was being used to clear the broken egg up?

_____

_____

44 Book 2   © Paddy Kinsale, 1974. Resource © Sarah Lindsay, 2016, Oxford University Press, 2016

UNIT 1 Extension

Name _____ Date _____

Making Pancakes When My Mother Was Out

What do you think Mum is going to say when she comes home?

• What does Mum do?

• What does Mum say?

• How do the children feel?

A Write five sentences to continue the story. Draw a picture.

_____

_____

_____

_____

_____

_____

Nelson Comprehension Resources and Assessment, Books 1 & 2 © Sarah Lindsay, 2016, Oxford University Press, 2016   Book 2 45

UNIT 1 Support

Name _____ Date _____

Where's Dad?

Dad wants to buy some vegetables.
Pleasure looks for her dad.
Pleasure isn't going to get scared.
Pleasure sees a present for Paul.
Pleasure and Dad go on the bus to the market.

Copy these sentences in the right order.

1 _____

2 _____

3 _____

4 _____

5 _____

Draw a picture showing what you think happens next.

46 Book 2   Nelson Comprehension Resources and Assessment, Books 1 & 2 © Sarah Lindsay, 2016, Oxford University Press, 2016

UNIT 1 Extension

Name _____ Date _____

Where's Dad?

A Think about the story *Where's Dad?*
Circle the correct answers.

1 Where does most of the story take place?

Pleasure's house   the bus   the market

2 Who is the main character?

Pleasure's dad   Paul   Pleasure

3 What happens?
Pleasure buys a present for Paul.
Pleasure gets lost.
Pleasure's dad can't decide what to buy.

B Have you ever been lost or felt very frightened?
Write some sentences about how you felt.

_____

_____

_____

_____

_____

_____

_____

_____

Nelson Comprehension Resources and Assessment, Books 1 & 2 © Sarah Lindsay, 2016, Oxford University Press, 2016   Book 2 47